from SEA TO SHINING SEA

IOWA

By Dennis Brindell Fradin

CONSULTANTS

Loren N. Horton, Ph.D., Historical Resource Development Program Coordinator,
State Historical Society of Iowa

Robert L. Hillerich, Ph.D., Professor Emeritus, Bowling Green State University;
Consultant, Pinellas County Schools, Florida

CHILDREN'S PRESS
A Division of Grolier Publishing
Sherman Turnpike
Danbury, Connecticut 06816

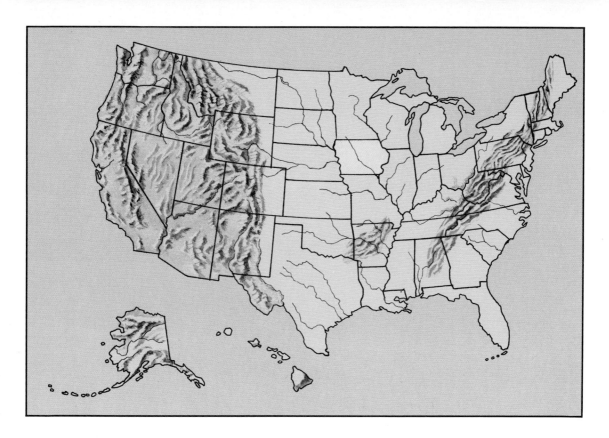

Iowa is one of the twelve states in the region called the Midwest. The other Midwest states are Michigan, Wisconsin, Illinois, Indiana, Ohio, Minnesota, Missouri, Nebraska, North Dakota, South Dakota, and Kansas.

For Clarence and Mabel Hill of Minburn, Iowa

Front cover picture: Town Clock Plaza, Dubuque; page 1: sunset at a Jackson County lake; back cover: Pikes Peak State Park

Project Editor: Joan Downing
Design Director: Karen Kohn
Research Assistant: Judith Bloom Fradin
Typesetting: Graphic Connections, Inc.
Engraving: Liberty Photoengraving

Library of Congress Cataloging-in-Publication Data

Fradin, Dennis B.
  Iowa / by Dennis Brindell Fradin.
    p. cm. — (From sea to shining sea)
  Includes index.
  Summary: Introduces the history, geography, industries, notable sights, and famous people of the Hawkeye State.
  ISBN 0-516-03815-X
  1. Iowa—Juvenile literature. [1. Iowa.] I. Title.
II. Series: Fradin, Dennis B. From sea to shining sea.
F621.3.F7 1993   92-16331
977.7—dc20   CIP
                                             AC

Sarah and Kelly Miller of Des Moines are all set to shovel snow.

Table of Contents

Introducing the Hawkeye State 4

"The Land Where the Tall Corn Grows" 7

From Ancient Times Until Today 13

Hawkeyes and Their Work 29

A Trip Through the Hawkeye State 35

A Gallery of Famous Hawkeyes 47

Did You Know? 54

Iowa Information 56

Iowa History 58

Map of Iowa. 60

Glossary 61

Index. 63

INTRODUCING THE HAWKEYE STATE

Iowa's people are called Iowans *or* Hawkeyes.

Iowa lies in the middle of the midwestern United States. The state was named for the Ioway Indians. One meaning for *Iowa* is "beautiful land." Iowa is called the "Hawkeye State." The nickname honors Chief Black Hawk. He was a great Sauk leader.

In the 1800s, thousands of farmers moved to Iowa. They planted crops in its rich soil. Today, the Hawkeye State helps feed the world. Iowa leads the other states at growing corn and raising hogs. It is also a top producer of soybeans, milk, oats, and sheep. Many factories in Iowa's cities package foods. Others make farm machinery.

Iowa has many other honors. Where were President Herbert Hoover and first lady Mamie Eisenhower born? Where were movie star John Wayne and newspaper writer Ann Landers born? What state is first in the percentage of people who can read? Where was the world's tallest corn grown? The answer to these questions is: the Hawkeye State!

A picture map
of Iowa

*Overleaf: Limestone
bluffs on the Upper
Iowa River*

"*The Land Where the Tall Corn Grows*"

"THE LAND WHERE THE TALL CORN GROWS"

*I*owa is in the part of the country called the Midwest. Six other midwestern states border Iowa. Wisconsin and Illinois are to the east. Missouri lies to the south. Nebraska and South Dakota are to the west. South Dakota also touches a small part of northern Iowa. Minnesota is Iowa's main northern neighbor.

Iowa covers 56,290 square miles. That makes it the twenty-fifth biggest of the fifty states. Most of its land is considered prairie. These flatlands contain some of the world's richest soil. Over nine-tenths of this land is farmland. Iowa has been called the "Land Where the Tall Corn Grows." In parts of Iowa, only cornfields and sky can be seen.

Iowa has no mountains. But the state's northeast corner is very hilly. Other places have low, rolling hills. A northwest Iowa farm has the state's highest point. It is 1,670 feet above sea level. Only

Only Nebraska, at 95 percent, has a higher percentage of farmland than Iowa, with 93 percent.

The Des Moines River in Ledges State Park

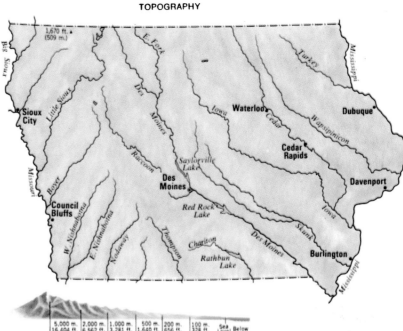

5,000 m.	2,000 m.	1,000 m.	500 m.	200 m.	100 m.	Sea
16,404 ft.	6,562 ft.	3,281 ft.	1,640 ft.	656 ft.	328 ft.	Level Below

ten states have a lower highest point. Iowa's lowest point is 480 feet above sea level. It is located in Keokuk.

Left: More than nine-tenths of Iowa's prairie is farmland.

RIVERS, LAKES, WOODS, AND WILDLIFE

The United States' longest river forms Iowa's eastern border. This is the 2,340-mile-long Mississippi River. The country's second-longest river forms most of Iowa's western border. This is the 2,315-mile-long Missouri River. The Big Sioux River flows along the rest of Iowa's western border. The Des Moines, Iowa, Cedar, Raccoon, Skunk, and Turkey rivers flow within Iowa.

9

A few artificially made lakes lie behind dams on Iowa rivers. One of them is Rathbun Lake, in southern Iowa. It is the state's biggest lake. Iowa also has many small natural lakes. They include Spirit, Clear, and Storm lakes.

The oak is Iowa's state tree. Maples, elms, cottonwoods, and hickories are also common. Colorful wildflowers brighten Iowa's prairies. They include violets, goldenrod, and sunflowers. The wild rose is the state flower.

The American goldfinch is Iowa's state bird. Cardinals, blue jays, bald eagles, and owls make their homes in Iowa. Ducks and geese are found there, too.

Deer roam Iowa's woods and fields. Raccoons and skunks also live there. Other wild animals include foxes, rabbits, and opossums.

CLIMATE

The weather plays an important part in Iowans' lives. Many of them are farmers. The weather can make the difference between a good harvest and a bad one.

Iowa averages about 30 inches of rainfall each year. Each winter Iowa receives about three feet of

Rabbits are among the animals that make their home in Iowa.

snow. But droughts can strike the state. Crops wither and die in these very dry periods.

Iowa tends to have hot summers and cold winters. January days often drop below 20 degrees Fahrenheit. In July, the state sometimes has days above 100 degrees Fahrenheit.

"Tornado Alley" runs through Iowa. This is an area down the middle of the country. Strong windstorms called tornadoes often strike there. In 1860, a tornado killed 200 people in Iowa and Illinois. Tornadoes also destroy buildings and crops.

Snow geese at De Soto Bend National Wildlife Refuge migrate south in the fall.

11

From Ancient Times Until Today

From Ancient Times Until Today

About 500 million years ago, shallow seas covered Iowa. Fossils of starfish have been found in the state. A big discovery was made in southeast Iowa in 1985. Scientists found amphibian fossils. They date back 355 million years. That was long before the first dinosaurs appeared. The amphibians looked like crocodiles. Scientists say they were relatives of today's birds and reptiles.

Two million years ago, the Ice Age began. Glaciers covered Iowa during that cold period. As these ice masses moved, they flattened Iowa's hills. Glaciers also spread rich soil across the land. Now this soil is Iowa's greatest treasure.

Giant beavers lived in Iowa during the Ice Age. They weighed about 350 pounds. Mammoths were there, too. These huge beasts were related to today's elephants.

American Indians

Ancient Indians reached Iowa at least 12,000 years ago. They hunted the mammoths and giant buf-

Opposite: A reenactment of a Civil War muster, Davenport

Amphibians are animals that live both in water and on land.

The glaciers were responsible for Iowa's rich soil.

faloes. About 3,000 years ago, American Indians began building mounds. They built hundreds of these dirt hills in Iowa. Most were burial places. Some were shaped like birds, bears, and lizards. Northeast Iowa's Woman Mound is 135 feet long. It is in the shape of a woman.

The Mesquakie Indians have a powwow every year at Tama.

The mound builders were related to more recent Indian groups. About twenty Indian groups lived in Iowa. One was the Ioway. Others were the Omaha, Oto, Missouri, Sioux, Illinois, and Ottawa tribes. The Mesquakies and Sauks came, too. Cities, rivers, and even states were later named for these American Indian tribes.

Over time, the Indians began to farm. They found that corn grew well in Iowa's soil. They also grew beans and squash. The Indians built villages near their crops.

The Indians generally lived along rivers. Trees along the rivers provided wood for their dome-shaped houses. They traveled by canoe along the rivers. In the spring, they planted corn. In the summer, they hunted deer and buffalo. While on hunting trips, they lived in tents called tepees. These cone-shaped tents were made of poles covered by animal skins. The Indians returned home in the fall to harvest their crops.

14

FRENCH EXPLORERS, TRADERS, AND SETTLERS

In the early 1600s, the French settled in eastern Canada. French explorers soon headed south into what is now the United States. In 1673, Louis Jolliet canoed down the Mississippi River. Father Jacques Marquette came with him. On June 25, they landed on the Iowa side of the Mississippi. Jolliet and Marquette were the first non-Indians to reach Iowa. The Indians warmly welcomed them.

French explorer La Salle canoed down the Mississippi past Iowa in 1682. He claimed land on

Father Jacques Marquette and Louis Jolliet (above) landed on the Iowa side of the Mississippi River on June 25, 1673.

La Salle's full name was René-Robert Cavelier, Sieur de La Salle.

15

both sides of the river for France. La Salle named the land Louisiana. Iowa was part of this claim.

French fur traders exchanged goods with Iowa's Indians. The Indians received blankets and kettles in return for furs. Beaver and other furs were made into clothing in France.

In 1754, England and France went to war over North America. England had thirteen colonies along the Atlantic Ocean. By 1762, France's cause was lost. In that year, France gave Louisiana to Spain. In 1763, England won the war. But England couldn't claim Louisiana. Spain owned it.

In the 1780s, the Mesquakies found lead in northeast Iowa. Lead was used to make gunshot. The Mesquakies began to mine the lead. In 1788, Julien Dubuque, a French-Canadian fur trader, arrived. The Mesquakies let him take over the mine. Dubuque also farmed. He became Iowa's first non-Indian settler. The town of Dubuque was later founded north of his home. Other French-Canadians arrived around the year 1800. They settled in present-day Lee and Clayton counties.

Also in 1800, Spain returned the Louisiana region to France. Spain had little interest in this land. Between 1762 and 1800, Spain had done nothing to settle Iowa.

Iowa Under American Control

In 1776, England's thirteen colonies declared themselves to be the United States of America. By the early 1800s, the new country wanted to expand west. In 1803, the United States bought Louisiana from France. Iowa was part of the Louisiana Purchase.

Iowa wasn't a state yet. It was just land claimed by the United States. First, Iowa was part of the Louisiana Territory. Later, it was part of the Missouri, Michigan, and then Wisconsin territories.

American explorers soon came to Iowa. William Clark and Meriwether Lewis pushed up along the Missouri River. They passed along Iowa's western

Below: The Lewis and Clark Expedition is reenacted.

Parading at Old Fort Madison

border in 1804. In 1805, Zebulon Pike's boats moved up the Mississippi River. Pike chose places along the river in Iowa for forts. An Iowa hill was named Pikes Peak for him. In 1806, he discovered the famous Pikes Peak in Colorado.

The United States Army built its first fort in Iowa in 1808. Called Fort Madison, it grew into the town of Fort Madison.

As American settlers moved west, the Indians lost their land. By 1830, most Sauks and Mesquakies had been pushed from Illinois to Iowa. Sauk chief Keokuk led Indians who accepted the move. But, in 1832, Sauk chief Black Hawk started a war. This was called the Black Hawk War. He hoped to return his people to Illinois. The Indians were defeated in the summer of 1832. Black Hawk lived his last years in Iowa. By 1851, most Indians had been pushed out of Iowa.

Settlers rushed to Iowa as the Indians left. They came by covered wagon, by horseback, and even on foot. These pioneers crossed the Mississippi River on flatboats.

The pioneers settled along rivers as the Indians had before them. Families chopped down trees near the riverbanks. They used the wood to build log cabins. River water was used for drinking and

The Black Hawk War was fought in Illinois and Wisconsin.

Sauk chiefs Keokuk (left) and Black Hawk (right)

bathing. Rivers also provided waterpower for mills in the new towns. Today, Iowa's ten biggest cities lie on rivers. The following cities were begun in the 1830s and 1840s: Des Moines, Cedar Rapids, Davenport, Waterloo, Iowa City, Dubuque, and Council Bluffs.

Iowa's pioneers planted corn, wheat, and oats. The crops grew well in Iowa's rich soil. Word spread that Iowa was great for farming. By 1840, Iowa was home to about 43,000 settlers.

Two years before, the Iowa Territory had been created. Iowa then had its own government. It was closer to statehood.

THE TWENTY-NINTH STATE

In 1846, Iowa's population reached 100,000. That was enough for statehood. On December 28, 1846, Iowa was made the twenty-ninth state. Ansel Briggs was the first state governor. Iowa City was the first state capital. Des Moines became the capital in 1857.

The new state grew quickly. From 1850 to 1860, Iowa's population more than tripled. It went from 190,000 to 675,000 people. Settlers kept coming from other states. People from Germany,

The Iowa State Capitol in Des Moines opened in 1884.

20

A Danish windmill at Elk Horn

Norway, Sweden, Denmark, and other countries also arrived.

Iowa and the rest of the northern states were "free states." This meant that slavery wasn't allowed. Landowners in the southern states, however, owned black slaves. Slaves did most of the work on the largest southern farms. Missouri, just south of Iowa, allowed slavery. Many slaves tried to escape from Missouri. They were fleeing to freedom in Canada. A secret network helped slaves escape northward. It was called the Underground Railroad. Many Iowans hid slaves escaping from Missouri. The Todd House at Tabor in southwest Iowa sheltered escaped slaves. It is thought that the slaves hid in a closet of the Todd House.

The clash over slavery and other issues led to the Civil War (1861-1865). It was fought between the Union (the North) and the Confederacy (the South). No battles were fought in Iowa. But almost 80,000 Iowans served the North. Grenville Dodge of Council Bluffs became a famous Civil War general. Mehitabel Woods carried food and supplies to the Iowa troops. The men called her "Auntie" Woods. In 1865, the North won the Civil War. That year slavery was ended in the United States.

An 1881 photo of the railroad station in Indianola

INDUSTRIAL AND AGRICULTURAL GROWTH

Before the Civil War, railroads linked towns in eastern Iowa. After the war, railroads reached across the state. By 1880, Iowa had 5,000 miles of railroad track. Only four states had more. No farm in Iowa was more than 25 miles from a train station. This helped Iowa farmers send their products to faraway markets.

In 1890, for the first time, Iowa led the states at growing corn. In the early 1900s, scientists taught farmers to grow new kinds of corn. They produced even bigger harvests. Corn meant so much to Iowa that a song was written about it in 1912. Schoolchildren were once taught the "Iowa Corn Song."

In 1910, Iowa plant scientists began growing soybeans from China. Soybeans grew well in the Hawkeye State. Iowa became a leader at growing them.

Also in the 1900s, manufacturing really got rolling in Iowa. In 1907, Fred Maytag began making washing machines. People called him the "Washing Machine King." His Maytag Company in Newton became a giant firm. Sheaffer is a famous pen company. It has been based in Fort Madison

This man was taking part in a 1901 corn festival.

since about 1913. Companies that made tractors and railroad cars also settled in Iowa.

WORLD WARS, WOMEN'S RIGHTS, AND DEPRESSION

In 1917, the United States entered World War I (1914-1918). About 113,000 Iowans served. About 2,000 of them died helping to win the war. Merle Hay of Glidden was one of the first American men killed. Marian Crandell was a French teacher from Davenport. She was the first American woman killed in the war zone.

American women had waged a long battle for the right to vote. They finally won the struggle in 1920. Carrie Chapman Catt and other Iowans helped win this victory.

Soon after they won the vote, Iowa women entered politics. Carolyn Pendray of Maquoketa made history in 1927. She became the first woman elected to the Iowa House of Representatives. In 1932, Pendray became the first woman elected to the Iowa Senate.

In 1929, Herbert Hoover, an Iowa native, became president of the United States. He was the thirty-first president (1929-1933). A few months

Carrie Chapman Catt worked hard for women's voting rights.

later, the Great Depression hit the country. Iowa farmers already owed banks much money. They needed loans for seed, tools, buildings, and land. The hard times of the Great Depression (1929-1939) made matters worse. A drought ruined Iowa's crops during the 1930s. Many farmers couldn't pay their bank loans. Thousands of Iowans lost their farms.

The coming of World War II (1939-1945) helped end the Great Depression. The United States entered the war in 1941. Iowa corn fed American troops. About 180,000 Iowa men and women helped win that war. The five Sullivan brothers from Waterloo joined the navy. They served together on the same ship. Their ship, the USS *Juneau*, was sunk in 1942. All five Sullivans died.

Nearly 6,000 Iowans died in World War II.

These students at Hampton took part in a World War II scrap-metal drive.

GROWTH AND CHALLENGES

By the 1950s, many Iowans started moving to cities. They took jobs in factories. Iowa reached a milestone in 1960. For the first time, more Hawkeyes lived in cities than on farms.

During the 1960s, John Hanson began making motor homes. People could both live and travel in this new kind of vehicle. Hanson named his motor home the Winnebago. Forest City is headquarters for the Winnebago Company. This town became the country's motor-home capital.

The lieutenant governor is Iowa's highest official after the governor.

In the 1980s, more women began holding government offices in Iowa. Jo Ann Zimmerman was a nurse. In 1986, she was elected lieutenant governor of Iowa. Zimmerman became the first woman in Iowa to hold that post. Also in 1986, Linda Neuman joined the Iowa Supreme Court. She was the first woman judge on the state's highest court.

Iowa farmers started having problems in the 1980s. Those years were like the Great Depression had been for their parents. The cost of farming rose. But the prices earned for farm goods did not keep pace. Many Iowans lost their farms. The farmers' troubles hurt industry, too. Companies that sold seeds and tractors lost business.

The farm troubles caused many Iowans to move elsewhere. Iowa's population dropped during the 1980s. It fell by about 126,000 people during those years. Many small farming towns in Iowa are having trouble surviving.

One point in Iowa's favor is its low jobless rate. By 1993, one American adult in every fourteen was out of work. But in Iowa, the jobless rate was half that number. Only Nebraska and South Dakota had lower jobless rates.

Iowa's leaders are working on ways to bring more companies to the state. In 1991, riverboat gambling started on the Mississippi. Many tourists visited the river towns of Davenport and Dubuque. People from other parts of the country have started to move to Iowa. They like the Hawkeye State's clean air and small towns.

The President *Riverboat Casino at Davenport brings many tourists to Iowa.*

The number of Iowa farms dropped from 120,000 in 1972 to 104,000 in 1990 to 100,000 in 1993.

Overleaf: A farmer near Waukon

Hawkeyes and Their Work

HAWKEYES AND THEIR WORK

The U.S. Census counted 2,776,755 Hawkeyes in 1990. Iowa has more people than twenty states, but less than twenty-nine states.

Of every 100 Hawkeyes, 96 are white. White Iowans trace their roots to all parts of Europe. Some towns hold festivals that honor their European background. Each spring, Elk Horn has a Danish festival. Decorah hosts a Norwegian festival each summer. Stanton hosts the Swedish Santa Lucia Festival at Christmastime. Children parade with lit candles as part of this holiday. Orange City and Pella hold spring tulip festivals. Dutch people from the Netherlands settled those towns.

There are only about 48,000 black Iowans. Yet black people have played a big role in the state. Grinnell College admitted both blacks and whites in 1860. George Washington Carver went to college in Iowa during the 1890s. He later taught at Iowa State University.

About 33,000 Iowans are Hispanic. Most of these people are from Mexico. About 7,000 American Indians live in the Hawkeye State. Many

The ancestors of most Iowans were European.

are Mesquakies. They returned to Iowa and bought land in Tama County in 1856.

HAWKEYES ARE SPECIAL

Isaac Galland opened Iowa's first school in 1830. It was near what is now Keokuk. Since then, Iowans have been well educated. Iowa has had a high literacy rate since 1880. Nearly all Iowans can read and write today. Of every 100 Hawkeyes, 85 finish high school. Iowa has one of the country's highest percentages of high-school graduates.

Literacy is the ability to read and write. Many experts rank Iowa first in literacy today. But some rank Utah first.

Many Iowans leave their cars and homes unlocked. Iowa has one of the country's lowest crime rates. Their peaceful life agrees with Hawkeyes. They live to an average age of seventy-six. Only Hawaiians and Minnesotans live longer.

Six of every ten Hawkeyes live in cities. Yet there is still a small-town feeling to Iowa. Most of Iowa's cities and towns have only a few thousand people. In many Iowa towns, just about everyone knows everyone else. This may account for Iowa's low crime rate and high level of education. It is hard to skip school in a town where everyone knows you! And good neighbors don't commit crimes against one another.

HAWKEYES ON THE JOB

Nearly 1.5 million Iowans have jobs. The state's most common kind of job is selling goods. About 300,000 Hawkeyes do this. The goods range from food to cars and tractors.

    Another 300,000 Hawkeyes provide services. Many are doctors, lawyers, and nurses. People who fix farm machinery are also service workers. About 220,000 Hawkeyes work for the government. Many of them are teachers in the public schools.

This man works as a radio station announcer at Iowa State University. He gives weather and farm reports.

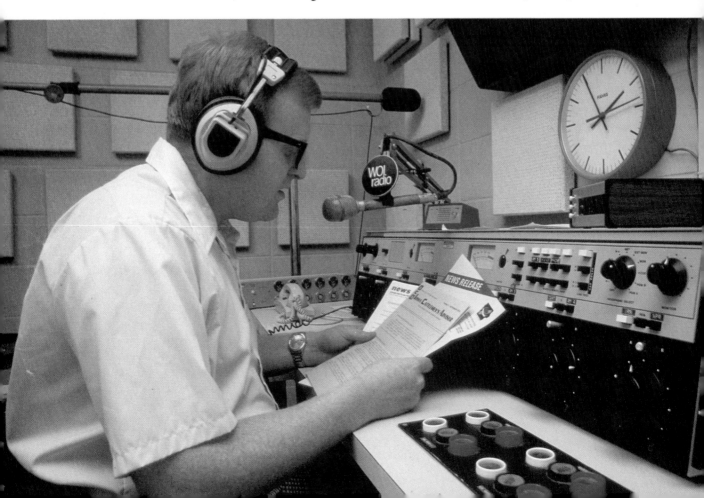

Left: Heritage Days is held in Walnut Grove Pioneer Village near Long Grove.
Right: A commercial fisherman on the Mississippi River at Lansing

About 125,000 Iowans are farmers. Iowa leads the country at growing corn. That is its top crop. Much of the corn is fed to livestock. It also goes into food for people. Corn flakes, corn chips, corn bread, and corn on the cob are a few of those foods. Iowa ranks second after Illinois as a soybean-growing state. Soybeans are used in salad dressings, margarine, and animal feed. Iowa is also a leader at growing oats and hay.

Iowa leads the states at raising hogs. There are about 14 million hogs on Iowa farms. That is five hogs per Iowan. Iowa is among the top ten states

for raising beef cattle and dairy cattle. Sheep, turkeys, and horses are also raised on Iowa farms.

About 235,000 Iowans make products. Iowa leads the country in packaging meat. Canned ham and breakfast sausages are important products. Quaker Oats has a plant in Cedar Rapids. It is the world's largest breakfast-cereal mill under one roof. Other foods made in Iowa include popcorn and corn syrup. Iowans also are top makers of tractors and other farm machinery.

Only about 2,000 Iowans are miners. They mine limestone, clays, and sand and gravel.

Iowa raises one-fifth of the country's corn, one-sixth of its soybeans, and one-fourth of its hogs.

Overleaf: A view of Cedar Rapids

33

A Trip Through the Hawkeye State

A Trip Through the Hawkeye State

*I*owa is a great place to visit. The state's farms and towns have a quiet beauty. Its few large cities are interesting but not too big. Some visitors take part in the Great Bicycle Ride Across Iowa. Nearly 7,500 riders pedal 460 miles. This week-long bike tour is held each summer.

Des Moines

Des Moines is Iowa's largest city. It lies where the Raccoon River empties into the Des Moines River. The city began as Fort Des Moines in 1843. It has been Iowa's capital since 1857.

The state capitol is a building with a golden dome. The Iowa legislature and the governor's office are inside. The governor lives in a big house called Terrace Hill. It is open to visitors.

Many people in Des Moines work for the government. Others are in the insurance business. Des Moines is one of the world's top five insurance centers.

Des Moines has exciting places to visit. The State Historical Building has many exhibits. A dis-

These cyclists are taking part in The Great Bicycle Ride Across Iowa.

The name Des Moines comes from the Indian word Moingona. *It may mean "river of the mounds," referring to Indian mounds.*

play on ecology is a favorite with children. The Science Center of Iowa has displays on space. Plays and concerts are performed at the Des Moines Civic Center.

The print shop at Living History Farms

Each spring, Des Moines hosts both the Girls and the Boys State Basketball Tournaments. In August, Des Moines holds the Iowa State Fair. It is one of the country's oldest and biggest fairs.

The Girls State Basketball Tournament is held in Des Moines.

Living History Farms are west of Des Moines. This outdoor museum shows how Iowa has changed over 300 years. An Ioway village shows how Indians lived around 1700. There is a pioneer farm of the 1850s and a farm from 1900. An 1875 town has homes, shops, and a church. Displays also explain how Iowa farmers work today.

Highlights of Western Iowa

Ames is just five miles southwest of Iowa's exact center. Iowa State University is in Ames. The school is famous for its farming programs. It also offers many other subjects. John Vincent Atanasoff was an Iowa State University scientist. He helped develop the computer in 1939.

Mamie Doud Eisenhower's birthplace is in Boone. It is a few miles west of Ames. Mamie was the wife of Dwight Eisenhower. He was the thirty-fourth president of the United States. Visitors can see the bed where Mamie Doud was born. Boone is also the site for a 15-mile railroad tour. The Boone

The Boone & Scenic Valley Railroad

& Scenic Valley Railroad rolls through lovely wooded hills.

Council Bluffs is southwest of Boone. It lies along the Missouri River. Council Bluffs began as a trading post and fort in the 1820s. Today, visitors can tour the General Dodge House in Council Bluffs. Grenville Dodge helped bring the eastern end of the Union Pacific Railroad to Iowa.

The Squirrel Cage Jail is another highlight of Council Bluffs. This three-story jail housed prisoners from 1885 until 1969. The cell block is round. Each floor has one door. The guard cranked the cell block around to the opening. Then a prisoner could be let in or out of a cell.

DeSoto National Wildlife Refuge is north of Council Bluffs. Snow geese and ducks fly along this part of the Missouri River. Autumn is the best time to see them.

Sioux City lies along the Missouri River in northwest Iowa. The town was founded in 1854. It was named for the Sioux Indians. Today, the city has about 80,000 people. It is Iowa's fourth-largest city.

The Sioux City Public Museum has displays on Iowa history and wildlife. The Sergeant Floyd Monument is a Sioux City landmark. Sergeant Charles Floyd died in 1804. He was part of the

The Squirrel Cage Jail in Council Bluffs (above) is one of only three that remain in the United States.

39

Lewis and Clark Expedition. Floyd was the first non-Indian known to be buried in Iowa. A 100-foot-tall monument marks his grave. The Floyd River of northwest Iowa was named for him.

West Bend is northeast of Sioux City. Visitors can tour the Sod House there. Western Iowa had few trees when the pioneers arrived. Some families cut up chunks of the ground. They piled up these dirt bricks to build sod houses. The Grotto of the Redemption is also in West Bend. The walls of this cave have nine scenes from the Bible. Father Paul Dobberstein spent forty-two years making them. He used rocks from many states and countries.

Northwest of West Bend is Spirit Lake. The Gardner Cabin and Museum can be visited there. The cabin was the only building left after an 1857 Sioux attack. About fifty settlers were killed. Fourteen-year-old Abigail Gardner survived. She later wrote a book about the Spirit Lake Massacre. She lived in the cabin.

South of West Bend is Fort Dodge. The fort was built in 1850 to protect settlers. Later, it became the city of Fort Dodge. Visitors can tour the building that looks like the old fort. Frontier Village is near the fort. It shows what a small plains village of the 1850s was like.

Highlights of Eastern Iowa

The Grotto of the Redemption, in West Bend

Waterloo and Cedar Falls are next-door neighbors. They both lie on the Cedar River. And they both were settled in 1845. Iowans call the cities Waterloo-Cedar Falls.

The Grout Museum is in Waterloo. The museum's Discovery Zone for children has science and history activities. Children can try on pioneer clothing.

The Ice House Museum is in Cedar Falls. It is an icehouse from early days. Early Iowans had no refrigerators. A block of ice in an icebox kept their food fresh. The people used ice that was cut in win-

Two views of the Old Capitol, in Iowa City

ter from the Cedar River. The ice was kept in the icehouse. There it lasted through the summer.

Cedar Rapids is on the Cedar River southeast of Waterloo-Cedar Falls. It is Iowa's second-biggest city. Settled in 1841, Cedar Rapids now has about 110,000 people.

Iowa artist Grant Wood taught school in Cedar Rapids. The Cedar Rapids Museum of Art has the largest collection of his paintings. One, *Young Corn*, shows an Iowa scene.

Brucemore is another highlight of Cedar Rapids. Visitors can tour this twenty-one-room mansion. One owner of Brucemore kept lions on the grounds. Grant Wood decorated the sunroom.

Iowa City is south of Cedar Rapids. It is on the Iowa River. Iowa City was founded in 1839 as the

Iowa Territory's capital. Iowa City was also Iowa's first state capital. The government met in the Old Capitol. Today, Iowa City is home to the University of Iowa. Its sports teams are the Hawkeyes. The Old Capitol is on the university's grounds.

About 30,000 students attend the University of Iowa.

The Amana Colonies are northwest of Iowa City. People from Germany founded these seven villages in the 1850s. Today, the Amana Colonies are Iowa's best-known tourist attraction. Visitors buy furniture, baked goods, and woolen cloth. Amana refrigerators are in many American homes.

West Branch is east of Iowa City. Herbert Hoover was born there in 1874. Visitors can enter

A furniture maker in the Amana Colonies

Snake Alley, in Burlington, is said to be the crookedest street in the world.

The bald eagle is the national bird of the United States.

the one-room cottage where he was born. The Hoover Library and Museum are also in West Branch.

Farther east is the Mississippi River. Many interesting Iowa cities have grown along its west bank. Keokuk is on the river at Iowa's southeast corner. Sauk chief Keokuk is buried in the city. The home of Samuel Miller is in Keokuk. President Abraham Lincoln named Miller to the United States Supreme Court. He served on it from 1862 to 1890. Today, his home is open to visitors.

Burlington is north along the Mississippi. The first American flag in Iowa flew over present-day Crapo and Dankwardt Parks. The town's Snake Alley is the crookedest street in the world. That is according to Ripley's *Believe It or Not.*

Davenport is Iowa's third-biggest city. It is up the great river from Burlington. Davenport was founded in 1836. It was named for fur trader George Davenport. The Putnam Museum has displays on Davenport history. Watching eagles is fun around Davenport. Some of the bald eagles have 8-foot wingspans.

Dubuque is up the Mississippi from Davenport. Dubuque was founded in 1833. It is named for Iowa's first non-Indian settler. A tower that looks

like a castle marks Julien Dubuque's grave. Iowa's oldest building is in Dubuque. The Arriandau log cabin was built before 1833. Near Dubuque is Crystal Lake Cave. It has rocks that look like animals and people. There is an underground lake in the cave.

Effigy Mounds National Monument is in northeast Iowa. It is a good place to end an Iowa tour. About 200 Indian mounds are in this part of Iowa. Some look like birds and other animals. Great Bear Mound is 137 feet long and 5 feet high. It is one of the largest animal-shaped mounds in North America.

President Herbert Hoover's office at the Hoover National Historic Site, in West Branch

A Gallery of Famous Hawkeyes

A Gallery of Famous Hawkeyes

Many Hawkeyes have become famous. They include the country's first woman lawyer and the "Father of Radio." Movie stars, baseball players, and artists have also come from Iowa.

Amelia Jenks Bloomer (1818-1894) was born in New York. She later lived in Council Bluffs. In 1849, she founded *Lily*. It was a magazine for and by women. Bloomer wrote about women's rights. She is best known for wearing "bloomers." These were baggy pants like pantaloons. Bloomer wore a skirt over the pants. This outfit gave women more freedom of movement.

William "Buffalo Bill" Cody (1846-1917) was born on a farm near Davenport. As a teenager, he rode for the Pony Express. This was a fast mail service in the West. Later, he became a famous buffalo hunter. Cody also formed Buffalo Bill's Wild West Show. It toured the United States and Europe.

Arabella Babb Mansfield (1846-1911) was born near Burlington. She studied law for two years in her brother's law office. In 1869, Mansfield became the country's first woman lawyer.

Opposite: President Herbert Hoover

William "Buffalo Bill" Cody

Carrie Chapman Catt was also principal of Mason City High School.

Charles Ringling

Carrie Chapman Catt (1859-1947) was born in Wisconsin. She grew up in Charles City, Iowa. She became a great fighter for women's rights. Catt helped women win the right to vote. She also founded the League of Women Voters. It informs voters about issues. Today, the league has about 100,000 members.

Charles Ringling (1864-1926) was born in McGregor. He and his brothers put on circus acts in their backyard. Under Charles's guidance, the Ringling brothers built the country's leading circus. It is called the Ringling Brothers and Barnum & Bailey Circus.

Kate Shelley (1866-1912) lived near Moingona. On July 6, 1881, a storm washed out a nearby railroad bridge. A railroad engine plunged off the bridge into the water. Fifteen-year-old Kate saw the washed-out bridge. She crawled over a 696-foot bridge above the Des Moines River. Railroad spikes cut her hands and knees. She told the station agent to stop another train that was coming. Shelley was awarded the state of Iowa's first medal for heroism.

U.S. presidents have a "cabinet." Its members head government departments. **James Wilson** (1835-1920) was from Iowa's Tama County. He

Left: Henry C. Wallace
Right: His son, Henry
A. Wallace

served in the cabinet longer than any other person. "Tama Jim" was secretary of agriculture for sixteen years (1897-1913). **Henry Cantwell Wallace** (1866-1924) was born in Illinois but lived in Iowa. His son, **Henry Agard Wallace** (1888-1965), was born on an Adair County farm. Father and son both served as U.S. secretaries of agriculture. Henry Agard Wallace also served as vice president of the United States (1941-1945).

Eugenie Moore Anderson was born in 1909 in Adair. She was a nursery-school teacher. Then she entered politics. In 1949, she was named ambassador to Denmark. Anderson held the post until 1953. She was the first U.S. woman ambassador.

Lee De Forest (1873-1961) was born in Council Bluffs. He did a great deal to develop radio. He became known as the "Father of Radio." De Forest also helped invent the "talkies." These were the first movies with sound.

John Wayne (1907-1979) was born in Winterset. He made about 200 movies. Many of them were cowboy films. His acting in *True Grit* won him an Academy Award in 1969. **Cloris Leachman** was born in Des Moines in 1926. She became a movie and television actress. Leachman won an Academy Award in 1971. It was for her role in *The Last Picture Show.*

John Wayne's real name was Marion Morrison.

Left: Cloris Leachman
Right: John Wayne

Grant Wood (1891-1942) was born on an Anamosa farm. He grew up there and in Cedar Rapids. For years, he tried to paint like European artists. He had little success. Finally, he realized: "All my really good ideas came when I was milking a cow." Wood began to paint pictures of Iowa scenes. He then achieved great fame. *American Gothic* is his most famous work. It shows a farmer and his daughter.

John L. Lewis (1880-1969) was born in Lucas. He headed the United Mine Workers' Union. Lewis helped millions of workers gain higher pay and better working conditions.

Grant Wood (above) used his sister and his dentist as models for American Gothic.

Anna Hedgeman

Adrian "Cap" Anson

Anna Arnold Hedgeman (1899-1990) was born in Marshalltown. She became a teacher and civil-rights worker. This black leader helped get the Civil Rights Act of 1964 passed. It protects the rights of black Americans.

Norman Borlaug was born near Cresco in 1914. As a plant scientist, he developed new kinds of wheat. They have helped feed people in many countries. For his work, Borlaug received the 1970 Nobel Peace Prize.

In 1918, twins were born into the Friedman family of Sioux City. They were named Esther Pauline and Pauline Esther. The Friedman twins did everything together. They were even married in a double ceremony. Later, both became newspaper advice columnists. **Esther Pauline** goes by the name **Ann Landers. Pauline Esther** is known as **Abigail Van Buren,** or **Dear Abby.**

The 1989 baseball movie *Field of Dreams* was filmed near Dyersville, Iowa. Many real-life baseball stars have been Hawkeyes. **Adrian "Cap" Anson** (1852-1922) was born in Marshalltown. He hit an amazing .339 in his twenty-seven-year career. **Bob Feller** was born in Van Meter in 1918. He began pitching in the big leagues when he was seventeen. Feller's 266 career victories included three no-hitters.

Children enjoy the work of **Stephen Gammell.**
Gammell writes and draws pictures for children's
books. He was born in Des Moines in 1943. In
1989, he won the Caldecott Medal. It was for his
pictures in *Song and Dance Man.*

*Twins Abigail Van
Buren (left) and Ann
Landers (right) at
their 50th high-school
reunion in Sioux City*

Birthplace of John Wayne, Anna Arnold
Hedgeman, Grant Wood, and Ann Landers . . .

Home to Black Hawk, Julien Dubuque, Amelia
Jenks Bloomer, and Carrie Chapman Catt . . .

The top state for growing corn, raising hogs,
and making farm machinery . . .

A state where nearly everyone can read . . .

This is Iowa—the Hawkeye State!

Did You Know?

In 1901, Iowa had nineteen straight days of temperatures 100 degrees Fahrenheit or hotter. In 1936, it had thirty-two days straight of temperatures 0 degrees Fahrenheit or colder.

A gingerbread house was built in Des Moines in 1988. It stood 52 feet high.

Lou Henry Hoover, President Herbert Hoover's wife, was born in Waterloo. She was national president of the Girl Scouts twice. In 1935, Lou Henry Hoover began the Girl Scouts' yearly cookie sale.

Le Mars, Iowa, may be the only town in the United States named for six women. The name was coined by stringing together the first letters from the names *Lucy, Elizabeth, Mary, Anna, Rebecca,* and *Sarah.*

Hooverball was invented in 1929 to keep President Herbert Hoover fit. The sport resembles volleyball but is played with a very heavy ball. Each summer, the Hooverball National Championships were held at Hoover's birthplace in West Branch.

Iowa has towns named Coin, Diagonal, Early, Gravity, Hawkeye, Morning Sun, and What Cheer.

There have been amazing instances of animals surviving Iowa tornadoes. A 1970 tornado at Radcliffe picked up a horse named Cheyenne Lady. She was blown a mile through the air and survived. A dairy cow near Davenport became known as Fawn the Flying Cow. Twice—in 1962 and 1967—tornadoes picked up Fawn and blew her through the air. Both times she landed unhurt.

Abraham Lincoln owned farms in Pottawattamie, Tama, and Crawford counties.

Des Moines native Phoebe Omlie bought an airplane when she was seventeen. She became a famous pilot in the early 1900s. She did air stunts for the movie series _The Perils of Pauline._ In 1929, she took a plane up almost 5 miles. That was a record for women pilots at that time.

The popular apple called "Delicious" was first grown in the late 1880s in an orchard near Macksburg.

George Reeves, star of the old "Superman" television show, was born at Woolstock. Jerry Mathers, who played Beaver in "Leave It to Beaver," was born in Sioux City.

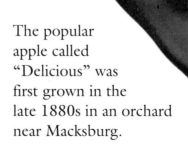

IOWA INFORMATION

State flag

Goldfinch

Wild roses

Area: 56,290 square miles (twenty-fifth among the states in size)

Greatest Distance North to South: 214 miles

Greatest Distance East to West: 332 miles

Borders: Wisconsin and Illinois to the east across the Mississippi River; Missouri to the south; Nebraska to the west across the Missouri River; South Dakota to the west across the Big Sioux River; Minnesota and a small part of South Dakota to the north

Highest Point: On a farm in northwestern Osceola County, 1,670 feet above sea level

Lowest Point: Only 480 feet above sea level, where the Mississippi and Des Moines rivers join at Keokuk

Hottest Recorded Temperatures: 118° F. (at Keokuk, on July 20, 1934)

Coldest Recorded Temperatures: -47° F. (at Washta, on January 12, 1912)

Statehood: The twenty-ninth state, on December 28, 1846

Origin of Name: Iowa was named for the Ioway Indians; one possible meaning of *Iowa* is "beautiful land"

Capital: Des Moines (since 1857)

Previous Capital: Iowa City (1846-1857)

Counties: 99

United States Representatives: 5 (as of 1992)

State Senators: 50

State Representatives: 100

State Song: "The Song of Iowa," sung to the melody of "Der Tannenbaum," words by Samuel H. M. Byers

State Motto: "Our Liberties We Prize and Our Rights We Will Maintain"

Main Nickname: "Hawkeye State"

Other Nicknames: "Corn State," "Corn-Hog State," "Land Where the Tall Corn Grows"

State Seal: Adopted in 1847

State Flag: Adopted in 1921

State Flower: Wild rose

State Bird: American goldfinch

State Tree: Oak

State Stone: Geode

Some Rivers: Mississippi, Missouri, Big Sioux, Little Sioux, Des Moines, Iowa, Cedar, Raccoon, Skunk, Turkey, Wapsipinicon

Some Lakes: Rathbun Lake, Lake Red Rock, Spirit Lake, Clear Lake, Storm Lake, Coralville Lake

Wildlife: Deer, raccoons, skunks, foxes, rabbits, opossums, squirrels, coyotes, chipmunks, rattlesnakes, American goldfinches, cardinals, woodpeckers, ducks, geese, bald eagles, owls, partridges, quails, pheasants, many other kinds of birds, bass, catfish, pike, walleyes, many other kinds of fish

Manufactured Products: Meat products, dairy products, breakfast cereals, other packaged foods, tractors and other farm machinery, construction machinery, tires and inner tubes, clothes washers and driers, pens, motor homes, chemicals

Farm Products: Corn, soybeans, oats, hay, alfalfa, rye, wheat, milk, hogs, beef cattle, dairy cattle, sheep, turkeys, chickens, horses, apples, cabbages, beans, onions

Mining: Limestone, clays, coal, sand and gravel

Population: 2,776,755, thirtieth among the fifty states (1990 U.S. Census Bureau figures)

Major Cities (1990 Census):

Des Moines	193,187	Iowa City	59,738
Cedar Rapids	108,751	Dubuque	57,546
Davenport	95,333	Council Bluffs	54,315
Sioux City	80,505	Ames	47,198
Waterloo	66,467	Cedar Falls	34,298

Oak tree (above) and oak leaves (below)

A geode with quartz crystals

Iowa History

10,000 B.C.—Ancient Indians reach Iowa about this time

1673—French explorers Louis Jolliet and Father Jacques Marquette explore Iowa

1682—René-Robert Cavelier, Sieur de La Salle, claims the Mississippi River valley for France and names it Louisiana

1735—French soldiers fight Sauk and Mesquakie Indians near what is now Des Moines

1762—Spain gains temporary control of French land west of the Mississippi, including Iowa

1788—Julien Dubuque, a French Canadian, becomes the first white man to permanently settle in Iowa

1799—French-Canadian Louis Honore Tesson settles near present-day Keokuk

1800—France regains control of Iowa and other lands from Spain

1803—As part of the Louisiana Purchase, the United States obtains Iowa from France

1804—Meriwether Lewis and William Clark move up the Missouri River along Iowa's western border

1808—The United States Army builds Fort Madison

1830—Dr. Isaac Galland opens Iowa's first school near what is now Keokuk

1832—Chief Black Hawk fights and loses the Black Hawk War

1833—Large numbers of settlers move to Iowa; the towns of Burlington, Dubuque, and Fort Madison are founded

1834—Iowa is made part of the Territory of Michigan

1836—Iowa becomes part of the Territory of Wisconsin

1838—On July 4, the Iowa Territory is created

1839—Iowa City is founded as the territory's capital

1841—Cedar Rapids is settled

1843—Fort Des Moines is built

1846—On December 28, Iowa becomes the twenty-ninth state

1855—The University of Iowa opens in Iowa City

1857—Iowans adopt a state constitution that is still in effect; Des Moines becomes the permanent state capital

1861-65—About 80,000 Hawkeyes help the North win the Civil War

1867—The first railroad across the state is finished

1868—Iowa State University opens at Ames

1874—Herbert Hoover is born at West Branch on August 10

1884—The state capitol is completed in Des Moines

1917-18—About 113,000 Hawkeyes help win World War I

1928—Herbert Hoover is elected the thirty-first president of the United States

1929-39—During the Great Depression, thousands of Iowa families lose their land

1940—Henry Agard Wallace is elected U.S. vice president with President Franklin D. Roosevelt

1941-45—About 180,000 Iowa men and women help win World War II; the five Sullivan brothers of Waterloo die when the USS *Juneau* sinks

1946—The Hawkeye State is 100 years old on December 28

1960—For the first time, more Hawkeyes live in cities than in farm areas

1970—Dr. Norman Borlaug wins the Nobel Peace Prize for developing new kinds of wheat

1989—An airplane crash near Sioux City kills 111 passengers, although many were saved by the skilled crew

1990—The U.S. Census counts 2,776,755 Hawkeyes

1993—Much of Iowa is devastated by the midwestern floods

1994—The 330 residents of Chelsea decide to move their homes to higher ground after suffering through 15 floods in the last 25 years

Iowa State University opened in Ames in 1868.

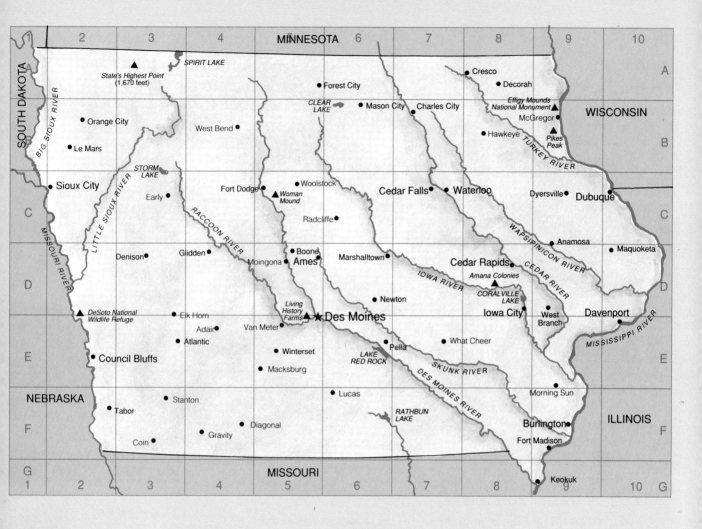

MAP KEY

Adair	E4	Decorah	A8	Iowa River	D7	Raccoon River	C,D4
Amana Colonies	D8	Denison	D3	Keokuk	G9	Radcliffe	C6
Ames	D5	Des Moines	E5	Lake Red Rock	E6	Rathbun Lake	F7
Anamosa	C9	Des Moines River	E,F7,8	Le Mars	B2	Sioux City	C2
Atlantic	E3	DeSoto National		Little Sioux River	C2	Skunk River	E7,8
Big Sioux River	A,B1,2	Wildlife Refuge	D2	Living History Farms	D5	Spirit Lake	A3
Boone	D5	Diagonal	F4	Lucas	F6	Stanton	F3
Burlington	F9	Dubuque	C9	Macksburg	E5	State's Highest Point	A3
Cedar Falls	C7	Dyersville	C9	Maquoketa	D10	Storm Lake	B,C3
Cedar Rapids	D8	Early	C3	Marshalltown	D6	Tabor	F2
Cedar River	D8,9	Effigy Mounds		Mason City	B6	Turkey River	B8,9
Charles City	B7	National Monument	B9	McGregor	B9	Van Meter	E5
Clear Lake	B6	Elk Horn	D3	Mississippi River	E9,10	Wapsipinicon River	C,D8,9
Coin	F3	Forest City	A5	Missouri River	C,D2	Waterloo	C7
Coralville Lake	D8	Fort Dodge	C5	Moingona	D5	West Bend	B4
Council Bluffs	E2	Fort Madison	F9	Morning Sun	F9	West Branch	D9
Cresco	A8	Glidden	D4	Newton	D6	What Cheer	E7
Davenport	E10	Gravity	F4	Orange City	B2	Winterset	E5
		Hawkeye	B8	Pella	E6	Woman Mound	C5
		Iowa City	D8	Pikes Peak	B9	Woolstock	C5

GLOSSARY

ambassador: A person who represents his or her government in another country

amphibian: An animal that can live both in water and on land

ancient: Relating to a time early in history

artificial: Made by people rather than occurring naturally

capital: A city that is the seat of government

capitol: The building in which the government meets

civil rights: The rights of a citizen

climate: The typical weather of a region

drought: A period when rainfall is well below normal in an area

explorer: A person who visits and studies unknown lands

fossil: The remains of an animal or plant that lived long ago

glacier: A mass of slowly moving ice

illustrator: A person who creates pictures for books and other printed materials

industry: A kind of business that needs many workers to make products

legislature: A lawmaking body

literacy: The ability to read and write

mammoth: A prehistoric animal that was much like today's elephants

manufacturing: The making of products

million: A thousand thousand (1,000,000)

monument: A building or statue that honors a person or famous event

motor home: A vehicle in which people can both live and travel

pioneer: A person who is among the first to move into a region

population: The number of people in a place

prairie: In its natural state, nearly level or rolling fertile land covered with coarse grasses and few trees

prehistoric: Belonging to a time before written history

reservation: Land in the United States that is set aside for American Indians

slave: A person who is owned by another person

tepee: A tent made of poles covered by animal skins and used by North American Indians

territory: Land that is owned by a country and that has its own government

tornado: A whirling windstorm from a funnel-shaped cloud that travels over land causing great destruction

Underground Railroad: A network of hiding places that helped slaves escape

union: A group that helps workers win higher pay and better working conditions

PICTURE ACKNOWLEDGMENTS

Front cover, © B. Vogel/**H. Armstrong Roberts;** 1, © Kevin Magee/**Tom Stack & Associates;** 2, **Tom Dunnington;** 3, © **Larsh K. Bristol;** 4-5, **Tom Dunnington;** 6-7, © **Tom Till;** 8, © **Tom Till;** 9 (left), © Dave Rusk/**N E Stock Photo;** 9 (right), **Courtesy of Hammond, Incorporated, Maplewood, New Jersey;** 10, © Sharon Cummings/**Dembinsky Photo Associates;** 11, © **Carl Kurtz;** 12, © Dennis Clevenger/**N E Stock Photo;** 13, © Craig Aurness/**H. Armstrong Roberts;** 14, © Vera Bradshaw/**Root Resources;** 15, North Wind Picture Archives, hand-colored; 17, © **P. Michael Whye;** 18, © Vera Bradshaw/**Root Resources;** 19 (left), **State Historical Society of Iowa;** 19 (right), **North Wind Picture Archives, hand-colored;** 20, © **Reinhard Brucker;** 21, © **Carl Kurtz;** 22, **State Historical Society of Iowa;** 23, **North Wind Picture Archives;** 24, **North Wind Picture Archives;** 25, **State Historical Society of Iowa;** 27, © Dennis Clevenger/**N E Stock Photo;** 28, © **Larsh K. Bristol;** 29 (top), © **P. Michael Whye;** 29 (bottom), © Dave Rusk/**N E Stock Photo;** 31, © **Cameramann International, Ltd.;** 32 (left), © Dennis Clevenger/**N E Stock Photo;** 32 (right), © **Larsh K. Bristol;** 33, © Robert Frerck/**Odyssey Productions;** 34-35, © **SuperStock;** 36, © **P. Michael Whye;** 37 (top), © **Reinhard Brucker;** 37 (bottom), © Vera Bradshaw/**Root Resources;** 38, © **Don Hennen;** 39, © **P. Michael Whye;** 41, © **Cameramann International, Ltd.;** 42 (left), © **P. Michael Whye;** 42 (right), © Doris De Witt/**Tony Stone Images;** 43, © **Cameramann International, Ltd.;** 44, © Bill Howe/**Photri;** 45, © Dennis Clevenger/**N E Stock Photo;** 46, Herbert Hoover, painting by Elmer W. Greene, © **White House Historical Association; photograph by the National Geographic Society;** 47, **AP/Wide World Photos;** 48, **Stock Montage, Inc.;** 49 (both pictures), **AP/Wide World Photos;** 50 (left), **Wide World Photos, Inc.;** 50 (right), **AP Photo Color;** 51, **AP/Wide World Photos;** 52 (both pictures), **AP/Wide World Photos;** 53, **AP/Wide World Photos;** 54 (bottom), **Variety Club of Iowa;** 54-55 (top), **Herbert Hoover Presidential Library-Museum;** 55 (bottom), **The Bettmann Archive;** 56 (top), **Courtesy Flag Research Center, Winchester, Massachusetts 01890;** 56 (middle), © Jansen/**H. Armstrong Roberts;** 56 (bottom), © Kitty Kohout/**Root Resources;** 57 (top), © **Jerry Hennen;** 57 (middle), © **Carl Kurtz;** 57 (bottom), © Mary A. Root/**Root Resources;** 59, **Iowa Department of Economic Development;** 60, **Tom Dunnington;** back cover, © **Carl Kurtz**

INDEX

Page numbers in boldface type indicate illustrations.

Amana Colonies, 43, **43**

Ames, 38, **59**

Anderson, Eugenie Moore, 49

animals, 10, **10, 11,** 39, 44, 55, **56,** 57

Anson, Adrian "Cap," 52, **52**

Arriandau log cabin, 45

Atanasoff, John Vincent, 38

Big Sioux River, 9

Black Hawk, 4, 18-19, **19**

Black Hawk War, 19

black people (African Americans), 21-22, 29

Bloomer, Amelia Jenks, 47

Boone, 38-39, **38**

Boone & Scenic Valley Railroad, 38-39, **38**

bordering states, 8, 56

Borlaug, Norman, 52

Boys State Basketball Tournament, 37

Briggs, Ansel, 20

Brucemore, 42

Burlington, 44, **44**

Carver, George Washington, 29

Catt, Carrie Chapman, 24, **24,** 48

Cedar Falls, 41-42

Cedar Rapids, 20, 33, **34-35,** 42

Cedar Rapids Museum of Art, 42

Cedar River, 9, 41-42

Civil War, **12,** 22-23

climate, **3,** 10-11, 25, 54, 56

Cody, William "Buffalo Bill," 47, **47**

computer, development of, 38

Confederacy (Civil War), 22

Council Bluffs, 20, 22, 29, **39**

Crandell, Marian, 24

Crapo and Dankwardt Parks, 44

crime rate, 30

Crystal Lake Cave, 45

Davenport, **12,** 20, 24, 27, **27,** 44, 55

Davenport, George, 44

De Forest, Lee, 50

De Soto Bend National Wildlife Refuge, **11,** 39

Decorah, 29

"Delicious" apples, 55

Des Moines, 20, **20,** 36-37, **37,** 50, 53, 54, 55

Des Moines Civic Center, 37

Des Moines River, **8,** 36

Dobberstein, Father Paul, 40

Dodge, Grenville, 22, 39

Dubuque, **Front Cover,** 16, 20, 27, 44-45

Dubuque, Julien, 16, 45

Effigy Mounds National Monument, 45

Eisenhower, Dwight, 38

Eisenhower, Mamie Doud, 4, 38

Elk Horn, **21,** 29

England, 16-17

ethnic groups and festivals, 20-21, 29-30, 43

explorers, 15-16

farming and farm products, 4, 8, **9,** 10, **13,** 14, 20, 21, 23, **23,** 25, 26-27, **28,** 32-33, **33,** 36, 37, 38, 55, 57

Feller, Bob, 52

fishing, 32

flag of Iowa, **56,** 57

Floyd, Sergeant Charles, 39-40

Forest City, 26

Fort Dodge, 40

Fort Madison, 18, **18,** 23-24

France and Frenchmen, 15-17

Frontier Village, 40

fur traders, 16, 44

Galland, Isaac, 30

Gammell, Stephen, 53

Gardner, Abigail, 40

Gardner Cabin and Museum, 40

General Dodge House, 37

geode (state stone), 57, **57**

geography of Iowa, 8-10, 56, 57

gingerbread house, 54, **54**

Girl Scouts, 54

Girls State Basketball Tournament, 37, **37**

Glidden, 24

government of Iowa, 20, 24, 26, 36, 42-43, 56

Great Bear Mound, 45

Great Bicycle Ride Across Iowa, 36, **36**

Great Depression, 25, 27

Grinnell College, 29

Grotto of the Redemption, 40, **41**

Grout Museum, 41

Hampton, **25**

Hanson, John, 26

"Hawkeye State," 4

Hawkeyes (sports teams), 43

Hay, Merle, 24

Hedgeman, Anna Arnold, 52, **52**

hills, 8, 13

Hispanic people, 29

history of Iowa, 13-27, 36-45, 58-59

Hoover, Herbert, 4, 24, 43-44, **46,** 54

Hoover, Lou Henry, 54

Hoover Library and Museum, 44

Hoover National Historic Site, **45**

Hooverball, 54, **54-55**

Ice House Museum, 41-42

Illinois, 8

Indianola, **22**

Indians (Native Americans), 4, 13-16, **14, 15,** 18-19, **19,** 29-30, 37, 39, 40, 44, 45

Iowa City, 20, 42-43, **42**

"Iowa Corn Song," 23

Iowa River, 9, 42

Iowa State Fair, 37

Iowa State University, 29, **31,** 38, **59**

Iowa Territory, 20, 42-43

Ioway Indians, 4, 14, 37

Jackson County, **1**

jobs, 27, 31-33, **31, 32,** 36

Jolliet, Louis, 15-16, **15**

Keokuk (Sauk chief), 9, 18, **19,** 44

Keokuk (town), 30, 44

lakes, **1,** 10, 45, 57

Landers, Ann, 4, 52, **53**

Lansing, **32**

Leachman, Cloris, 50, **50**

Ledges State Park, **8**
Le Mars, 54
Lewis, John L., 51
Lewis and Clark Expedition, 17-18, **17,** 40
life, Iowans' length of, 30
Limestone Bluffs, 6-7
Lincoln, Abraham, 44, 55
literacy, 4, 30
Living History Farms, 37, **37**
Long Grove, **32**
Louisiana Territory, 16-17
Mansfield, Arabella Babb, 47
manufacturing, 4, 23-24, 26, 31, 33, 57
maps of Iowa showing:
 cities and geographical features, **60**
 location in U.S., **2**
 products and history, **4-5**
 topography, **9**
Maquoketa, 24
Marquette, Jacques, 15-16, **15**
Mathers, Jerry, 55
Maytag, Fred, 23
Mesquakie Indians, 14, **14,** 16, 18, 29-30
Miller, Samuel, 44
mining, 33, 57
Minnesota, 8, 30
Mississippi River, 9, 15, 18, 19, 27, **32,** 44
Missouri, 8, 21
Missouri River, 9, 17-18, 39
Morrison, Marion (John Wayne), 50
motor homes, 26
museums, 37, **37,** 39-40, 41, 42, 44
name, origin of, 4, 56
Nebraska, 8, 27
Neuman, Linda, 26
Newton, 23

nicknames, Iowa's, 4, 57
Old Capitol, **42,** 43
Omlie, Phoebe, 55
Orange City, 29
Pella, 29
Pendray, Carolyn, 24
people of Iowa, 20-21, 29-33, **29**
Pike, Zebulon, 18
Pikes Peak, 18
Pikes Peak State Park, **Back Cover**
pioneers, 19-20, 37, 40, 41
plants, 10, 29, **56, 57**
population, 20, 27, 29, 30, 39, 42, 57
prehistoric Iowa, 13-14
products of Iowa, 4, 23-24, 32-33, **32, 33,** 57
Putnam Museum, 44
railroads, **22,** 23, 24, 38-39, **38**
Rathbun Lake, 10
Reeves, George, 55, **55**
Ringling, Charles, 48, **48**
riverboat gambling, 27, **27**
rivers, 9, 10, 14, 15-16, 17, 19-20, 27, 36, 39, 40, 41, 42, 44, 57
schools, 29, 30, **31,** 38, 43, **59**
Science Center of Iowa, 37
Sergeant Floyd Monument, 39-40
service industries, 31
settlers, 16-21, 40, 44
Shelley, Kate, 48
Sioux City, 39-40, 55
Sioux City Public Museum, 39
Sioux Indians, 14, 39, 40
size of Iowa, 8, 56
slavery, 21-22
Snake Alley, 44, 44
Sod House, 40
South Dakota, 8, 27
Spain, 16

Spirit Lake, 40
sports, 37, **37,** 43
Squirrel Cage Jail, 39, **39**
Stanton, 29
state capitol, **20,** 36, **42,** 43
State Historical Building, 36-37
state symbols, **56,** 57, **57**
statehood, 20, 56
Sullivan brothers, 25
Tabor, 21-22
Tama County, 30, 48
Terrace Hill, 36
Todd House, 21-22
topography of Iowa, **9,** 56, 57
tornadoes, 11, 55
town names, unusual, 54
trees, 10, 14, **57**
Underground Railroad, 21
Union (Civil War), 22
Union Pacific Railroad, 39
University of Iowa, 43
Upper Iowa River, 6-7
Van Buren, Abigail, 52, **53**
voting rights, 24, 48
Wallace, Henry A., 49, **49**
Wallace, Henry C., 49, **49**
Walnut Grove Pioneer Village, **32**
Waterloo, 20, 25, 40, 41, 54
Wayne, John, 4, 50, **50**
West Bend, 40, **41**
West Branch, 43-44, **45**
Wilson, James, 48-49
Wisconsin, 8
Woman Mound, 14
women, 24, **24,** 26, 47, 48, 49, 50, 52, **52, 53,** 55
Wood, Grant, 42, 51, **51**
Woods, Mehitabel, 22
world wars, 24-25, **25**
Zimmerman, Jo Ann, 26

ABOUT THE AUTHOR

Dennis Brindell Fradin is the author of 150 published children's books. His works for Childrens Press include the Young People's Stories of Our States series, the Disaster! series, and the Thirteen Colonies series. Dennis is married to Judith Bloom Fradin, who taught high-school and college English for many years. She is now Dennis's chief researcher. The Fradins are the parents of two sons, Anthony and Michael, and a daughter, Diana. Dennis graduated from Northwestern University in 1967 with a B.A. in creative writing, and has lived in Evanston, Illinois, since that year.

DEMCO